Texas, My Texas

by Roger T. Moore

Great Texas Line Press
Fort Worth, Texas

Texas, My Texas

For bulk sales
and wholesale inquiries
contact:
Great Texas Line Press
Post Office Box 11105
Fort Worth, TX 76110
greattexas@hotmail.com
www.greattexasline.com
817-922-8929

To see our complete list of Texas guidebooks, humor books and cookbooks, visit greattexasline.com.

Cover design: Kari Crane
Editor: Amy Culbertson
Cartoons: Roger T. Moore
Book design: Tom Johanningmeier

Great Texas Line Press strives to be socially responsible, donating a portion of proceeds from several books to Habitat for Humanity of Fort Worth, North Fort Worth Historical Society, Texas Dance Hall Preservation Inc. and Terlingua's Big Bend Educational Foundation. Hundreds of books are donated annually to public radio stations throughout Texas for fund-raising. Every effort is made to engage Texas writers, editors, illustrators, designers and photographers who fell victim to the newspaper industry crisis.

Introduction

Roger T. Moore and his cartoons could brighten the outlook of an about-to-be-lynched horse thief, not to mention providing a smile for anyone else who flips through one of his ongoing series of Texas History Calendars or follows him in one of the many weekly newspapers that publish his cartoons.

A Texas living treasure, Merkel rancher, family man, civic leader and Will-Rogers-like philosopher-humorist, Moore has been penning cartoons since the 1970s, getting funnier and funnier each year. Some would call him an artist, but he sees himself simply as a guy with a sense of humor who draws.

He has been producing his Texas history calendar since 1998 and has 25 newspapers running his weekly Lone Star cartoons. Not only do they make you laugh, the cartoons make a point, each amounting to a visual mini-editorial administered with equal doses of Texas facts and trivia.

So why does Moore think up a cartoon a week? Well, it ain't about the money.

First, since Texas has a lot of colorful history, looking for his brand of "I'll be danged, I didn't know that" subject matter, or for aspects of our past that are just plain humorous, is the kind of research he finds fulfilling.

Second, given that most people are not exposed to a lot of our state's history, he likes spreading the word to other Texans and those elsewhere in the world who'd like to get here as soon as they could.

You're going to enjoy looking at this collection of Moore's best cartoons.

– Mike Cox, Austin

Mike Cox is author of Wearing the Cinco Peso: A History of the Texas Rangers 1823-1900 *and 23 other Texas-related books.*

Our Texas jackrabbit can top 45 mph for short distances ... a "hare" slower than a racing horse.

Feb. 14, 1854: The first telegraph office in Texas opens in Marshall.

Texas is the fourth-leading state for the production of pumpkins.

April 28, 1900: The Southwest Sacred Harp Singing Convention is founded ... it was appreciated by a "higher-up."

Our little opossum is immune to the poison of Texas snakes.

July 4, 1883: The first recorded rodeo is held in Pecos ... one event, Tag Team Bronco Ridin', never caught on.

April 20, 1836: The "Twin Sisters," identical cannons given to Texas by Ohio sympathizers, are used for the first time.

A horse born in Jacksboro lived 47 years ... that's 143 in human terms. Pony Boy died in 1957.

In the early '70s, Texas A&M (who else?) institutes a one-of-a-kind fish medicine program.

Dec. 10, 1928: A big bundle of joy named Dan Blocker is born in DeKalb. He would star in "Bonanza" as Hoss Cartwright.

Seagraves carbon plant workers used to get overtime **pay** for showering before they went home.

Scientists in Agglieland once tried to create a square egg, citing shipping efficiency, etc. ...

The Texas Angus Leasing Co. of Houston once leased cows for $500 per year.

Only two native Texans signed the Declaration of Independence ... Francisco Ruiz and Jose Navarro.

Jan. 17, 1929: Popeye the Sailor is born in a comic strip by Elzie Crislar Segar in the *Victoria Advocate* newspaper.

Jan 20, 1891: Gov. James S. Hogg is inaugurated as the first native Texan governor.

Jan. 22, 1973: Texan George Foreman knocks out Joe Frazier to win the heavyweight title.

Jan. 28, 1960: Dallasites Clint Murchison and Bedford Wynne receive an NFL franchise for a team they name the Cowboys.

The Permanent School Fund is set up by the Legislature in 1854 to fund Texas' public schools and universities.

Feb. 10, 1910: D.L. McDonald, the father of irrigation on the Texas High Plains, finds water near Hereford.

Feb. 19, 1846: During the Texas Annexation ceremony, the final lowering of the Lone Star flag results in a broken flagpole.

Feb. 19, 1846: The Republic of Texas is officially declared at an end.

Feb. 21, 1943: Women Airforce Service Pilots (WASP) trainees arrive at Avenger Field near Sweetwater, making it the first coed flight school in the United States.

Feb. 26, 1888: The less-than-beautiful Goddess of Liberty is placed atop the state Capitol.

The foundations for the U.S. Air Force are laid in San Antonio's Fort Sam Houston in 1910 by a gutsy pilot named Benjamin Foulois, flying the Army's first military plane.

March 2, 1910: The first U.S. military pilot makes his first solo flight at Fort Sam Houston. Orville and Wilbur Wright – via correspondence – are the flight instructors.

March 6, 1836: The Alamo falls.

And ...

March 6... the day the Alamo fell.
It didn't fall. it's standin' up right in th' middle of downtown San-tone!
ROGER MOORE ©'01

March 16, 1861: Gov. Sam Houston refuses to take the oath of allegiance to the Confederate States of America.

March 24, 1891: Electric lights are authorized for the state Capitol.

April 14, 1958: Texas pianist Van Cliburn wins the first Tchaikovsky International Competition in Moscow.

April 19, 1685: The LaSalle Expedition records the first surgery in Texas. The victim was bitten by a rattlesnake and died.

April 21, 1836: The Mexican Army is so confident that they don't even post guards at San Jacinto. They are completely routed by Sam Houston's army.

April 21, 1941: Sam Houston's 86-year-old son, Andrew Jackson Houston, is appointed U.S. senator.

June 21, 1857: Charles Alderton is born. As a pharmacist in Waco in 1885, he would concoct a famous carbonated beverage.

April 29, 1936: The town of McCamey holds the first "Rattlesnake Derby."

May 17, 1835: A.B. Dodson marries Sarah Bradley. She later gives him a "Lone Star" flag for his army company.

May 13, 1839: A brig that was originally loaded with 150 tons of ice from northeast rivers arrives in Galveston Harbor.

May 18, 1977: Millionairess Sandra West is buried inside her blue 1964 Ferrari in a San Antonio cemetery.

May 23, 1541: Coronado gives thanks for friendly Indians in Palo Duro Canyon.

June 3, 1965: Texan Ed White takes the first American space walk.

June 15, 1937: Country singer Waylon Jennings is born in Littlefield.

June 16, 1838: John Quincy Adams begins a three-week filibuster in the U.S. House of Representatives against the annexation of Texas.

Sept. 27, 1948: Texas' first TV station, WBAP in Fort Worth, goes on the air with a speech by President Harry Truman.

June 23, 1931: Native Texan Wiley Post begins his first flight around the world.

July 8, 1907: Post, founded as Post City by C.W. Post of "Toasties" fame, becomes the Garza County seat.

July 12, 1912: Katherine Stinson, who would soon start a flight school in San Antonio, gets her pilot's license. Despite her fame as a pilot, she is rejected by the military because of her gender in World War I.

Feb. 3, 1836: A volunteer militia from Alabama called the "Red Rovers" (for their bright-red pants) joins Texas' fight for independence.

July 13, 1944: Bombers from Biggs Field in El Paso accidentally dump their dummy bombs on Sierra Blanca in West Texas.

Feb. 8, 1836: The famous Davy Crockett arrives to entertain and defend at the Alamo.

July 18, 1979: Gale Burr of Irving claims the record for the longest mustache in Texas: 2 feet.

July 25, 1882: Judge Roy Bean opens his first saloon west of the Pecos.

July 28, 1933: W.E. Morris becomes the first Texas farmer paid to plow under his crop.

July 1976: The country's first clothing-optional apartment complex opens in (where else?) Austin.

Aug. 1, 1918: Emma Banister in Coleman County becomes the first female sheriff in the United States.

Aug. 2, 1973: The infamous Chicken Ranch in La Grange ceases operations.

December 1777: French engineer Luis Andry and his crew begin mapping the Texas-Louisiana coast all the way to Matagorda Bay.

Oct. 6, 1897: William Brann, editor of the crusading magazine *The Iconoclast*, is beaten in Waco by three men (one was a judge) for daring to criticize Baylor University.

Sept. 18, 1861: John B. Stetson designs the first real cowboy hat – an immediate hit with the Texas Rangers.

Sept. 20, 1973: Billie Jean King, 29, beats Bobby Riggs, 55, in the "Battle of the Sexes" tennis match in the Astrodome.

Sept. 25, 1830: The first Texas law against gambling is enacted.

Oct. 3, 1981: Gov. Bill Clements declares the armadillo the official mascot of Texas.

Nurseryman A. E. Henninger of McAllen finds a red mutation of a pink grapefruit in 1929 and develops it into the Ruby Red grapefruit.

Oct. 24, 1932: Plennie Wingo of Abilene completes his 8,000-mile trip of walking backward around the world.

Oct. 25, 1931: The famous Texas Prison Rodeo is born.

Nov. 5, 1878: Fresh out of prison, notorious gunfighter Johnny Ringo is elected constable of Loyal Valley.

Nov. 13, 1857: Frederick Dawson of Baltimore contracts to build six vessels for the second Texas Navy.

Nov. 10, 1991: Texas' most beloved cartoonist, Ace Reid, dies. But his art lives on. His famous strip, "Cowpokes," still creates smiles all over the Lone Star State and beyond.

April 22, 1897, Houston: Sarah Seelye becomes the only woman ever accepted into the Grand Army of the Republic.

Nov. 24, 1874: Joseph Glidden patents an improved double-strand barbed wire.

Dec. 2, 1854: Texas grants David Crockett's widow $24 for "services at the Alamo."

Dec. 20, 1993: Gussie Nell Davis, founder of the Kilgore Rangerettes, dies at 87.

Dec. 23, 1927: A gunman dressed as Santa leads robbers in the heist of a Cisco bank.

April 23, 1936: Roy Orbison is born in Vernon. He would get his first guitar at age 6.

The nine-banded armadillo, our official state small mammal, always has four offspring, always genetically identical.

April 21, 1836: After the San Jacinto battle, Santa Anna tried to disguise himself.

Famous black cowboy Bill Pickett from Taylor invented bulldogging: His method involved biting the animal's upper lip to help subdue and upend the victim.

May 11, 1894: George Dahl is born. In 1938 as a Texas-based architect, he would design the nation's first drive-through banking facility in Dallas.

1932, Big Spring: A California tourist is cited by local police for "indecent exposure" for wearing shorts.

May 27, 1957: Buddy Holly and the Crickets release their first single, *That'll Be the Day*.

June 26, 1832: Texans defeat the Mexican army at Velasco, a prelude to war.

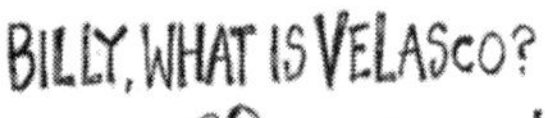

July 4 is celebrated by Texans as Independence Day. We also celebrate March 2: Texas Independence Day.

July 17, 1938: Refused clearance to fly from New York to Dublin, Galveston's "Wrong Way" Corrigan ostensibly heads back to Los Angeles. He arrives in Dublin 23 hours later, citing a broken compass.

Dec. 25, 1839: Famous frontiersman Kit Carson carves his name on a boulder in the Davis Mountains.

Up to 200 Texas historical markers are added yearly, though not all applications are approved.

July 24, 1893: Josephine Lucchese is born in San Antonio. Her father is famous bootmaker Sam Lucchese.

Dec. 12, 1884: With barbed wire having chopped up the open range, a cattleman's convention proposes a one-mile-wide "Cattle Highway" to drive herds northward.

Oct. 30, 1836: John R. Jones is appointed Texas' first postmaster, at a time when mail delivery is dangerous and unreliable.

A Texas law still on the books mandates that no one can carry pliers that could be used to cut a fence.

The film industry's biggest award may have been nicknamed for Oscar Pierce, a Texas farmer. He was related to the film academy's first librarian, who said the statuette reminded her of her "Uncle Oscar."